# Poems To Shape Lives

# Poems To Shape Lives

## Inspirational Verse on the Gospel, Life, Love, and Family

Joseph D. Rees

Illustrated by

Travis Crowther

*INTERNATIONAL STANDARD BOOK NUMBER*
*0-88290-059-5*

*LIBRARY OF CONGRESS CATALOG CARD NUMBER*
*76-3993*

Printed in the
United States of America
by

HORIZON
PUBLISHERS

Post Office Box 490
55 East 300 South
Bountiful, Utah 84010
292-1959

I would to write
some simple verse
to tell a tale or two.
I would to help men
phrase their thoughts
and voice a point of view.

I would to write
inspiring words,
unveiled from all disguise.
I would to draw
men nearer God
with words serene and wise.

I would to write
assuring words,
for those who would to see
That love goes on
beyond the grave
and through eternity.

I would to write
some tranquil verse,
to raise one's thoughts above.
I would to write
for those who speak—
for those who pray—and love!

To

My Lovely Wife

Elaine

# Contents

*Love and Family*



*On the Light Side*

# The Gospel and God

# Eternal

Eternal are the truths here taught
upon our mountain sod.
Eternal are the precepts learned.
Eternal is our God.

Eternal does the Judgment last,
Once Judgment's passed, my friend,
Though heaven and earth may pass away,
Eternal has no end.

Eternal are the blessings given.
Damnation is the same.
Eternally God does His work.
Eternal is His name!

# I Would To Visit Bethlehem

I would to visit Bethlehem,
its ancient ruins worn.
I would behold the sacred place
where Jesus Christ was born.

I would to see the ancient inn,
where Mary sought to lie,
the barn where wise men followed there
a star within the sky.

And then I'd visit Nazareth,
where, as a boy was seen
the One the prophets had foretold
would be a Nazarene.

To see the tiny village there,
where Jesus learned and grew,
law on law and word on word,
might teach me something too.

And next I'd visit Galilee
and stroll its peaceful rim,
where Jesus asked the fishermen
to come and follow Him.

To visit such a sacred place,
forsake all thoughts of care,
I'd well imagine it was now
and maybe see Him there.

The Garden of Gethsemane,
I would to visit then,
where Jesus took upon His soul
the punishments of men.

Where there He shrank to drink the cup,
but did, despite all care.
No man can yet conceive how much
our Savior suffered there.

At last, perhaps, I'd look around,
perchance the hill to find,
where Jesus gave His mortal life
to resurrect mankind.

I would behold, in reverent peace,
so far across the sea,
perhaps to more appreciate
what Jesus did for me!

# Worthwhile Moments

There comes to each
throughout the day
those moments filled with wonder,
those robust times of work and play.
Some schedule each within the day,
and many waste their lives away—
seeking nothing fonder.

For life is vain
for us on earth
when recklessly we wander.
While all attempt to live from birth
a life of riches, ease and mirth,
the wise will seek out times of worth,
—times to pray and ponder.

# Try And Then Decide

Life, we wonder
what thou art,
plan or blunder
from the start.
Well conceived,
the master plan!
Or is to be
whatever can?

Or is existence
just for fun?
Better had it
not begun,
than find no purpose
here for man!
Each must judge
the best he can.

Savior's mercy
finds a way,
or *can* the night
be turned to day?
Many theories
meet the test,
so only conscience
judges best.

Peace or sorrow,
joy or pain
comes tomorrow
once again,
but what about
beyond this life,
father, brother,
sister, wife?

Truth and error
will impart,
leaving footprints
on the heart.
You decide
what you will be,
to stay, for all
eternity.

Is man to reap
what he does sow?
Is the Gospel
true, or no?
The Holy Spirit
will confide.
Try it out
and then decide!

# Not Doubting

Unstable—uncertain
as clouds in the sky,
as dew on the heather,
as storms drawing nigh.

Doubting—suspecting
what yet to believe.
Learning to conquer,
compare and conceive.

Learning of wisdom
and truth to be sure,
things as they will be
and things as they were.

As weak as a candle
in the cool morning breeze,
as foilage in Autumn
forsakes all the trees,

But growing, in winter,
through trials of worth,
strong roots ever deeper
inside of the earth.

Certainty forming,
as buds on the flower,
in spring-time to blossom,
wider each hour,

With fragrance and beauty
and long-lasting love.
Drawing the spirit
of truth from above,

Until last, in summer,
when skies are all blue,
to know then, not doubting,
the Gospel is true!

# Proselyte

I look
   and wonder there
why I
   should even care.
We talk
   of clouds and rain,
war, floods,
   of peace and pain.
Then I,
   with growing trust,
know then
   I only must
assume
   the arduous task.
Stop, think,
   then finally ask.

There is a book
   an iron rod.
There is a heaven.
   There is a God!
Now look here, Joe.
   It's true, you see.
So will you come
   to Church with me?

Rolling drum
   within my chest,
pounding hard
   at such a quest.
Breathe a sigh,
   my conscience rid,
knowing, well
   at least, I did.
Waiting still,
   encourage some,
'till at last
   he says, "I'll come!"

# A Search For Heaven

A fair young lad
  of nearly seven,
left home one morn
  to search for heaven,
but not quite certain of the way,
  knelt down upon his knees to pray.

'Twas early morn,
  the stars still shined,
the hills still hid
  their dawn behind.
A small clear stream he knelt beside
  and, pure in faith, asked God to guide.

This small brave lad
  roamed far that day
and felt that God
  did lead the way.
Through meadow and wood that boy did rove,
  thought not of home, nor of its love.

He'd ventured far,
  or so did seem,
thought not to turn,
  but followed his dream
and deep in a wood he asked his God
  how close to heaven he had trod.

He yet walked on,
  though dusk was nigh,
knew not his place,
  so dark the sky,
o'er hill and field that day did pass,
  then knelt to rest in tall green grass.

Asleep he fell
   and dreamed of heaven,
of God and earth,
   this lad of seven
awoke next morn and found his bed
   had a small clear stream near its head.

That same small stream
   he had knelt beside
that morn before
   and asked God to guide.
So this lad, the answer given,
   realized then, he'd found his heaven.

Heaven from men
   is not set apart.
Tranquility dwells
   within one's heart.
This brave young boy took true advice,
   "Don't seek, but *make* your paradise!"

# How Soon?

How long, Father, must it last,
 the night, till endless day?
As through the cold and sightless dark
 thy chosen children disembark
to find the right amidst the wrong,
 their voices rising ask, "How long?"

How far, Father, will it be,
 the bright and endless shore?
When on the cloudy, storm-tossed sea
 thy faithful children look to Thee
as navigation from a star.
 Their prayers ascending ask, "How far?"

How high, Father, will they be,
 the waves that we must ride?
When icy limbs are turning numb
 we pray for strength to overcome;
to better mount them in the sky
 we would Thou tell us, yes, "How high?"

"How near, Father, are we now?"
 Thy children pray to know.
Amidst this dark and loathsome fuss,
 we would Thou calm the seas for us
and facing life with doubt and fear,
 we wonder, Father, yes, "How near?"

How soon, Father, are they o'er,
 the trials that men must face?
Though through temptation all must grow,
 but still Thy children would to know,
so cry at midnight, morn and noon
 to learn of Thee, our God, "How soon?"

# To Me

*The Me of Yesterday*

Oh wretched man that I have been,
 my soul's at war with thee
and, rife with hate, I promulgate
 to you my emnity!

For you have caused my grief to swell
 in coals of conscience, flames of hell.
Too well I know that I must see
 your wretched face eternally.

*The Me of Today*

Oh sleeping man that in me dwells,
 would I your sleep surcease
and teach your eyes to recognize
 it's love that wins you peace;

For you are apt to grudge and hate.
 God help me help you renovate.
Today you work to bring to me
 tomorrow's full felicity.

*The Me of Tomorrow*

Oh shapeless mass of blood and clay,
 I sketch, then chip you some,
and at this rate, I postulate
 on what you will become.

Of you I dream and think and pray.
 I shape and carve you every day,
reforming then, incessantly,
 to mold of you, tomorrow's me!

# Obey!

Mine eyes have spanned the mountainsides,
traversed the salty sea,
beholding desolations and untold misery;
where are the wicked sinners, who righteousness downtrod,
adulterous and corrupted, the enemies of God.

Mine ears have heard the endless cry
that judgment's brought them there,
too proud to bow before our God in humble earnest prayer,
and heard within the darkest nights the dying sinner's moan,
for he who sins, when death begins, encounters her alone.

My nose has smelt the sickening stench,
where corpses do decay,
where God has dealt with evil men, who mocked His righteous
But God, He hath no pleasure in the death of them that die.
Though God is kind, He's also just, can n'er His laws defy.

Mine hands have touched the gravestones there,
where evil men are laid,
who for the evil deeds they've done are being justly paid
by suffering through eternity in chains of mournful rue.
Bemoaning of their filthiness is all they'll ever do.

My mind, it ponders of the realm
where prophets have inferred
no human eye has ever seen, nor human ear has heard,
nor human heart can comprehend, nor human tongue can say
what blessings God has stored for those who hearken and obey

# Holy Writ

My breast does fast
within me burn,
to see a child
to the scriptures turn,
to read the writ of holy men,
to seek direction there again
and comprehending every word,
follows counsel from the Lord,
whose words are just and true and plain.

And then I see, with saddened eyes,
these "learned men,"
who but surmise
amongst themselves the livelong day
on what the prophets "meant" to say
and in their quest to follow through
the word of God, they misconstrue
and from His Spirit doth take away.

So thus these men,
who think they're grand,
don't even really
understand
why, how long, or what to do,
and leading others with them too,
as blind leads blind into the ditch,
they fall, not knowing which is which
of right or wrong or false or true.

And so I would
those holy men
might visit earth
and preach again,
to find these tales and set them straight,
their feeble fables extricate,
while the Judge, Himself, with robe and gavel,
before mankind the *truth* unravel,
to free men thus and end debate!

# Hearken

Oh House of Israel, sons of Jacob,
your God, who dwells on high,
doth summon you from every nation,
kingdom, power and generation,
accepting no one's disputation.
Hearken! Lest ye die!

Oh House of Israel, sons of Isaac,
the evening's drawing nigh.
Your God would then that ye would hear Him,
praise His works and always fear Him,
obeying always, drawing near Him.
Hearken! Lest ye die!

Oh House of Israel, sons of Abram,
I fain would ask ye why
ye would to leave the God who loves you,
choosing he who would but shove you
in the ditch and rise above you?
Hearken! Lest ye die!

Oh House of Israel, sons of Noah,
your God doth breathe a sigh
and would that ye would mix with leaven,
repent and enter into heaven,
where eternal life is given.
Hearken! Lest ye die!

# It's Not The Swift

It's not the swift that win the race,
nor the battle to the strong,
but he that works the will of God
each day his whole life long.

While many justify their works
and the words of prophets bend,
the true *conform* to righteousness
each day up through the end.

Though men may put their trust in man
and in the flesh be sure,
it's not the swift that win the race,
but he that shall endure!

# Free To Choose

You may say "Son, have a drink!"
but I'll say "No, not me"!
For men who are the happiest
are those who still are free.

So have a drink or have a smoke,
a gift of friend or brother.
Have one now and maybe soon
another and another.

But friend, it's never just the threat
of health that one may lose,
But men who are the happiest
are those still free to choose.

Satan planned at first, you see,
before we now recall,
to take away our agency
and vowed to save us all.

So once again here now below
he would to take it still,
that we might not do the things we want,
but do the things we will.

So have a smoke or have a drink
and soon your life is spent
with time for smokes and time for drinks
but no time to repent.

For soon you lose your agency
and need one thing in life,
to find out where you lost your dough
and why you lost your wife.

But still a smoke, still a drink
to help you get along.
No one's hurt, but you my friend,
so what can there be wrong?

Then have a smoke or have a drink,
if yet you would but lose,
but men are still the happiest
who still are free to choose!

# A Prayer Was Said

A prayer was said demanding
a favor of the Lord.
A saint in goodly standing
upon his knees commanding
deserved the blessing's granting,
until His heart was stirred.

A prayer was said in sorrow
and begged the Lord to save.
While time was sought to borrow
a clean and white tommorow,
repentance born from sorrow,
and surely heaven gave.

A prayer was said believing,
while sins were all confessed,
and never once deceiving
the faith of yet receiving,
ungodliness bereaving,
the saint was surely blessed!

# Jerusalem

Oh Jerusalem, Jerusalem, thy cobblestones are worn!
How many prophets died in thee?
How many prophets born?
How many good men trudged the way
to seek thee from afar?
How many good men left thy gates
to fight for thee in war?
How many times, when thy arms were weak
thy God hath made them strong?
How many times has He gathered thee
as a hen would do her young?

Oh Jerusalem, Jerusalem, all day in vain repose,
how many times, thy head, held high,
saw not beneath thy nose?
How many good men in thy gates
hast thou scourged and hung for nought?
How many times hast Shiloh come,
whose death thy silver bought?
How many times hast thou been called
to partake of the wedding feast?
How many times must the Bridegroom call
e're thou shalt hear, at least?

Oh Jerusalem, Jerusalem, Thy Savior offered wine.
How many times to the wedding feast
hast thou been called to dine?
How many times did He pour the balm,
e're last thy bottles burst?
How many times hast thou paid the price?
How many times been cursed?
How many times has the battle raged
and thy sons and daughters fair
been dragged away to far off lands
to serve the heathen there?

Oh Jerusalem, Jerusalem, cursed is thy sod,
because thou scourged the prophets true
and crucified thy God!
How many days will come and go
e're thou shalt turn aside
to the Holy One of Israel
and be Jehovah's bride?
How many hours, Jerusalem,
do still, at last, remain
till thou shalt hear the words He speaks,
so simple, just and plain?

Oh Jerusalem, Jerusalem, the seed of Abraham,
how many times wilt thou sacrifice
in vain, the paschal lamb?
How many prophets have been called
to mark thy way before?
How many prophets MUST THOU SEE?
How many prophets more?

# Who Am I?

Tired and thirsty,
in need of life's bread,
eyes turned to heaven,
"Oh help me!" he said.

"God, up in heaven,
I know that you're there.
Please hear this one humble
vagabond's prayer."

And when it was answered,
eyes turned to the sky
asked God up in heaven
"Who am I? Who am I?"

That Thou should'st take time
up in heaven so vast
to answer a prayer
so helplessly asked

By one yet so worthless
and low, neath the sky?
Who am I, that Thou hearest?
Who am I? Who am I?"

Hours still later,
met a man on the way
weak, hungry and ill,
who only could say,

"Please brother, come help me!
My wife is back home
in need of some substance.
Please, brother, come

And give her some food, then,
that maybe she'll live.
Give of your substance.
Please, brother, give!"

He looked in his knapsack,
as a cupboard, near bare,
but gave what he had
to his poor brother there

And helped him back home
to his near dying wife,
that maybe his substance
might spare yet her life,

And did all he could
'till at last he was sure
that all was at right,
both for him and for her.

So back on the road,
in need of life's bread,
eyes turned to heaven
"Oh help me!" he said.

And when it was given,
asked God, in the sky,
"Who am I, that Thou hearest?
Who am I? Who am I?"

# Were All His Servants

Armies, guns and atom bombs
  are built to guard our border.
Within our ranks
  the armoured tanks
  now keep the peace and order,

While yet the prophets of our God
  are still His words preserving.
There is none here
  with cause to fear
  were all His servants serving!

# Omission

My heart, it dreads the judgment day,
   just like most everyone,
but less, because of things I did,
   as those I haven't done,
like kneel each night, in secret prayer
   or find the time to read
or visit all the sick I know
   or to good council heed;

like never break the Sabbath Day
   or always volunteer;
strengthen all the weak around
   and, to the saddened, cheer;
like testify to all the world
   there is a living Lord;
teach, expound His Gospel truths
   and guide men heavenward;

or be patient with the youth I know
   and to their level reach
and illustrate, with all I do,
   every word I teach;
or moderation in all things
   I eat or drink each day;
guide my mind in every thought
   or idle word I say.

If I forget my ancestors
   I'll suffer endless rue!
For we'll all bewail, as the bad we've *done*,
   the good we *didn't* do!

# Before The Cleansing

I searched, with torment tearing
my sorry soul apart,
to find the deepest ocean,
to cleanse my sinful heart.

I searched throughout the country
a river deep and wide,
to wash away my sorrows
and all my memories hide.

I looked into the heavens
and prayed for rain all year,
but God sent only showers
when I was never near.

While all was shameful sorrow
and day was dark as night,
no water 'neath God's heaven
could change my wrong to right.

I searched throughout the country,
found wisdom's bright array,
which taught there be repentance
before the cleansing day.

# The Death Of Joseph Standing

T'was a torrid summer morn.
The sun's effulgent rays were worn
upon the shoulders of a valiant two.
Joseph Standing, man of pride
with Rudgar Clawson, near his side
had travelled far, away from home,
to Georgia's meeting, held in Rome.
As missionaries they would go.
No purse nor script were they to know.
Not even food did they take along,
or guns, to save them from the throng
of sinful cowards, who had vowed
secret threatenings, evil, proud.
On their way with hasty stride
the cheerful comrades, side by side,
encountered round the trail's bend
men on horseback, none a friend,
for in their eyes the two could see
malice, hate enmity
and evil plans.
What now?

There in the heat that summer day
they marched those faithful two away
to do a deed so low of men
that Satan laughed a laughter then
of peevish glee.

They stopped to rest, where none would know,
and beat them till their blood did flow
and seethe upon the Georgia ground
More came riding, near the sound
when Joseph jumped (anoble ruse)
and cried "Surrender!" to confuse
the mob of villians on that day
to sieze the chance to run away.

But one sick fiend, too cold to scare,
took aim and shot poor Joseph there.
The shrapnel searing through his head,
Joseph Standing faltered, dead.

"Shoot! " young Rudgar then exclaimed,
to whom all weapons then were aimed.
Serene within the midst of hate
he folded his arms to boldly wait.
"Shoot! and let me die, as he,
or let me go where there might be
a man to help me to attend
to what remains here of my friend."

Alone, this boy, mid grief, disgust,
tenderly cleansed what would be dust,
but hours before had been his friend
and Christ's deciple to the end
and cringed, to pull back out that day
the lead that put his friend away.

With the westbound freight, his friend sent home,
on went Rudgar—on to Rome.

# Storm Clouds

I like to think, when I see a host of clouds
 cluster before a storm,
that God has just been weeping
and has filled with tears His soft, pillowy tufts of down
 to their highest level of saturation
 and the time has come to wring them.
I am sure, as His omnipresent eyes
 look down, they see much on this earth
 over which to weep, the pain and sorrow of suffering,
 the heartache that comes from the separation
 of death—and, most of all, sin
 and the base desires of the hearts of men.
 He moans, to see men form their secret plots
 to destroy their enemies, their friends
 and even their brethren, for He knows
 they will only be destroying themselves.
He bows His head to see wars, feuds and hate
 grow from grudges over petty things
 soon to be forgotten and,
when He sees a young boy
 or little girl take their first step
 down the road of selfishness
 that leads to carnal sin and self-
 destruction—He weeps.

There comes a time
 when every child does so, and I suppose
He's shed at least a tear or two
 for us all. Some, more than others,
 for His omniscient mind knows
 who of us shall not return.
Them he also loves; even enough
 to let them go.
Thus, as the days
 grow shorter and the time of harvest
 is near, as wickedness grows more common,
you may depend also
 on more rain, more clouds and summer showers.

But rejoice when the sun
breaks through, for it is then that another soul or two
have begun their long trek
up high cliffs and over rocky ridges,
up the mountain, home.
And be assured—that God is smiling.

# I Would Proclaim!

He rose again!
He rose again!
I would proclaim to you!
T'was Jesus, the Anointed One,
God gave the glory to.

It was the Christ,
the crucified,
who did, at last, atone,
who recompensed for Adam's sin
and many of our own.

Upon the cross
they hung Him up,
in humiliating gall,
but naked, wounded, spit upon,
He rose above us all.

The Wonderful,
The Councilor,
The Prince of Peace, on earth.
The hosts of heaven sang, in anthems,
rejoicing at His birth.

And the hosts of heaven
wept, beholding,
and held, as one, their breath,
as our Redeemer died, a ransom,
to break the bands of death.

Two days and nights,
t'was in the tomb,
His body that was slain.
But on the morning of the third
He conquered all disdain.

He rose again!
He rose again,
who man's redemption gives!
I would proclaim to all the world
that Christ, our Savior, lives!

# If Only I

Before the wood,
beyond the field,
the clouds will open wide
and yield
the heaven's face,
the angel's tree
and soon
the human race
will be
immortal souls,
as one with sky.

And oh I hope
that maybe I
will see that day;
no more concealed,
the heavens open wide
and yield
the Savior's work,
His greatest plan.
If only I
could be there then!

# Lessons from Life

# The Suicide (A Reading)

A man's prestige
Is weighed in wealth;
Success is backed by gold.
This life he brings
To win these things,
But then this story's told.

I lived in wealth
And knew in health
That life was sweet and kind.
And truth I thought
Is what men sought
But not what men could find.

I lived life well
As men could tell
From out the very start.
For all could see
Quite vividly,
A girl had won my heart.

The joy, the joy, the warm free joy
Was overcoming care;
But I promised rings
And worldly things
To prove my love was there.

"Oh life," I said,
"Is for the dead
If wealth has not a part.
I'll give my dear
Her wishes here,
Then surely own her heart."

The wealth, the wealth, the high
  cold wealth
Was fabricating fools;
For her love, they thought
My gold had bought,
Was only for some jewels.

I loved her then,
Though all the men
Had claimed they loved her too;
But mine was real,
And I could feel
That hers was also true.

Well, all went right
Though try men might
to criticize our love,
For I could see
Our destiny
Was set by God above.

But wealth, I still
Believed was strength
To give my life its goal;
But never thought
These things I sought
Could ever buy my soul.

The gods, the gods, the scoffed
  mad gods.
Were castigating fools;
For their lives were spent
And they'd ne'er repent
Though all had broken rules.

The Lord had planned
To break the land
That then was rich in gold;
But left their wealth
And took their health,
Worth more than sums untold.

The sky, the sky, the mad black sky
Was prophesying death;
And the heavens scowled
While the cold winds howled
Their lonesome gasp for breath.

My fate had cast
The die at last
When all had seemed at right.
I thought I'd won
But found her gone
Upon our wedding night.

The plague, the plague, the cold
    cruel plague
Was innovating grief;
For it took my love
To the gods above,
Just stole her like a thief.

For on that night I saw the light
Grow dim within her room;
Then felt her breath
Grow cold with death—
And heard the thunder boom.

The grief, the grief, the deep
    sad grief
Was reminiscing bliss;
For my love was dead
And I felt the dread
Of losing that last kiss.

A man's prestige
Is all his friends,
For friends he values high;
And gold he'll reap
His friends to keep,
But gold won't hold them nigh.

My friends all left
My side that night,
Their backs to me they turned;
For felt I cursed
And reimbursed
For all the wealth I earned.

"Oh life," I said,
"Is for the dead
Once love has lost its glow."
So then I wrote
The farewell note,
So all the world might know.

The note, the note, the short sad
 note
Was eulogizing death;
For my friends were dear
And I made it clear
That none of them were left.

Oh, 'twas all right
Until that night
When life began to pain;
But couldn't meet
The harsh defeat,
So drove myself insane.

The reef, the reef, the sharp cold
 reef
Was extripating chance;
For the cliff was high
And I wished to die,
To save our youth's romance.

Those lips were warm
That night of storm
When kissing me farewell;
I felt her breath
And swore my death
Would free my soul from hell.

The ride, the ride, the fast cold
  ride
Was militating sense;
For the reef was near
And I'd see my dear
At even life's expense.

And with the speed
Of my best steed
I felt the road grow long;
With every stride
I hummed inside
The funeral marching song.

The trees, the trees, the long
  armed trees
Were unifying ghosts;
And the road lay bare,
Only I was there
To see those God-sent hosts.

Fear gripped my brain
Within the rain
While riding there that night;
For every cloud
Would only shroud
A sure successful plight.

The plan, the plan, the mad
  cruel plan
Was putrifying thought;
For the reef was bare
And I called it there
"My suicidal spot."

A man's beliefs
Rule all his moves
Though seem they dark as night,
For chooses he
His destiny
By what he thinks is right.

The fear, the fear, the deep cold
fear
Was superceding thought;
For nobody cared
And the world just dared
Fate, to complete her plot.

"Oh, God," I prayed,
"Too long I've stayed
And felt this anguished fear;
For fate has left
My world bereft
And life is not so dear!"

"Oh take me God!
Thy lightning rod
May strike upon this ledge,
And end my life
Without a strife,
For I have made my pledge!"

The shame, the shame, the deep
mad shame
Was alleviating grief;
Than a suicide
I felt inside
'Twas best to die a thief.

"You fool!" I cried,
While deep inside
I felt the heaven's stare;
"You pray to God
For a lightning rod
To wipe away all care!"

"You know you'll find
No peace of mind
With death that holds no pride
So live, my friend
Until the end
And make no suicide!"

Each man himself
Will seek the truth;
Decisions rule his fate;
But when to find
He's changed his mind,
It may be then too late.

The cliff stood there
Untouched with care;
Behind he heard a crack;
So turned to see—
The sky fall free,
While cold rocks pierced his back.

A man's prestige
Is all his friends,
But this is not success;
Perhaps relate
The work of fate
To each man's happiness.

A man's prestige
Is his beliefs,
When these he calls his pride,
But man has yet
To ne're regret
Attempting suicide.

# Had I But Seen

Had I but seen our countrymen, two hundred years ago,
I would have joined them in their ranks
to fight against the foe.

I would have seen George Washington, upon a snowy day,
unmount his steed at Valley Forge,
in silence there to pray.

Had I but felt the brilliant minds, who nobly then gave birth
to the constitution of our Land,
the freest land on earth,

It would be men like Jefferson or Hancock that I'd seen,
perhaps a little more to know
what liberty does mean.

Had I but been with Paul Revere, upon that famous night,
I too would warn the minutemen
to arm themselves to fight.

Or had I been in Boston then, I would have joined with glee
the Indian raid upon the ship
to spoil ten tons of tea!

Oh had I seen the noble men, who died for freedom's birth,
perhaps I'd better understand
what liberty is worth.

Had I but seen our countrymen, two hundred years ago,
I proudly would have joined their ranks
to fight against the foe!

# Lucifer

She saw him off with sobbing eyes,
Sarah, filled with dread.
Mike promised he wouldn't climb that mount
again, once they were wed,

But fifteen years had come and gone.
Michael's heart did burn,
for the climbing fever beckoned him
and challenged his return.

For since he was a little boy,
Michael's mountain wailed
its deadening dare unto those who would
to climb its cliffs, but failed.

Michael was the first in town
scaled its ridgy rim.
Though it once was called "Old Lucifer,"
they named it after him.

Thrice he had made it to the top.
All the village stared,
amazed at the many mighty feats
that Michael even dared.

But "Michael's Mountain" tempted him,
"Lucifer" the same.
As the winds were whistling down, he thought
they challenged yet his fame.

He heard its cry throughout the field
to know if yet he can.
Though he once was young and strong and brave,
was now a married man.

"Look," he told her upon that night,
"It only takes a day
to reach the throne of old Lucifer.
I won't come back that way,

For on the other side you see
no cliffs with which to cope,
To descend back down from off the top
is just a gradual slope!

I'll be back in just two days.
Don't you worry so!
There's just one more thing that I must prove
so Lucifer will know."

Michael left and two days passed.
Misfortune foiled fame
and Sarah worried throughout the night,
for Michael never came.

They never found him on that mount,
nor saw him from that day,
nor does the mount yet bare his name.
He'd have it now that way.

A tombstone white, depicts his grave,
though no one there was lain,
while above it stands "Old Lucifer,"
the prince of death and pain!

# Peace

Life offers peace, my friend,
to those who have no foe,
no reason to contend,
no love to cherish so,
no freedom to preserve,
no cause to doubt or mourn,
no honor to deserve
from battles that are born.

May peace be given, friend,
to those who want no strife;
who'd rather not contend
than learn the worth of life;
who'd rather feel no love,
no heart or mind possess,
and pray for peace above
than fight for happiness.

Let peace be theirs, my friend,
but honor's born from strife;
and freedom must contend
to keep its treasured life;
and love has its desires
upon which discords grow,
whose conflict's crackling fires
both heat and light bestow.

Yes—pray for peace, my son,
but mind—our way of life
from battle has been won—
not peace—but endless strife!

## Our Actions Tell

I threw a scroll into the air.
It fell to earth, I knew not where.
Enclosed were words, no secret then,
that told the love I have for men.

I found a scroll, the other day.
From whence it came, I cannot say.
But oh those words, a joy to see,
they told of someone's love for me!

And like the scroll, our actions tell
our love for others, just as well.
Then, as our love's conveyed to men,
so shall it be—returned again!

# Tragedy

We watched upon the TV screen,
   the hero's vengeful killing.
We watched him rob the city bank,
   a feeling we call "thrilling."
We watched the hero every night
   a different woman wooing.
We watched him plunder, steal and fight
   or whatever he was doing.
But not a time did he get caught,
   nor did we want him, ever.
So, as he lived and killed and fought,
   he met with justice never.

Now when we meet the crowds each morn
   and in the traffic waiting,
we find our hearts with vengeance torn
   and the guy beside us hating,
because upon the TV screen
   the hero, he was joying,
when last he found "true happiness"
   by killing and destroying.

So, as we leave our beds each day
   to do our push and shoving,
we find we've lost the will to pray,
   incapable—of loving.

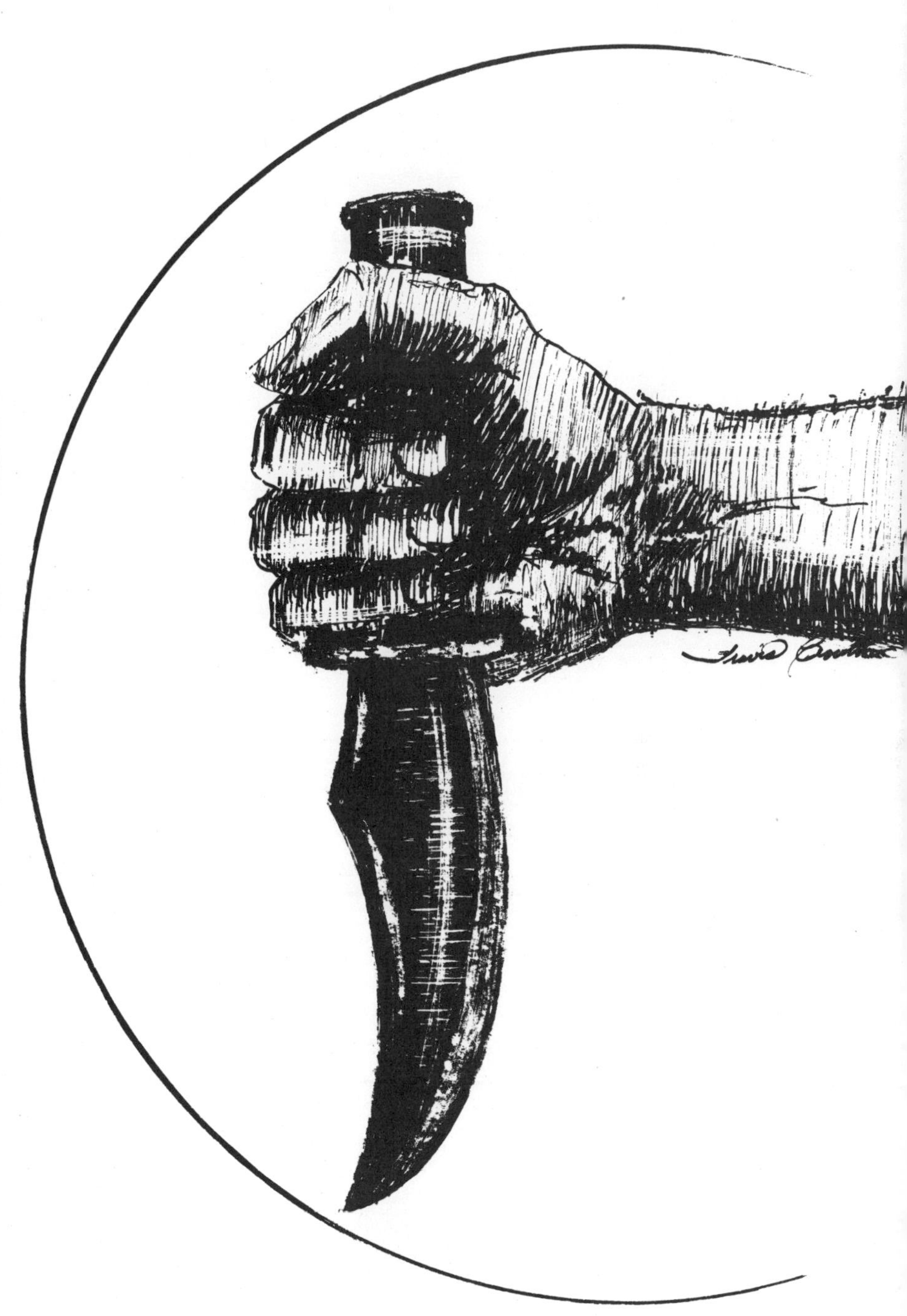

## The Sea

Many men, in fathoms tossed,
remind us of the victory, lost
because they fought for wealth and pride
against its timeless ebbing tide.

But, someday, men shall seek for bliss
and things of worth, like truthfulness,
and in the sea's deep darkness find
eternal truth and peace of mind.

## War Is Hell!

From out the grey Hawaiian sky
 soaring bombers, drawing nigh
 below the clouds, descending still.
At last there falls a roaring shrill
 with the boom of bombs, exploding near,
 erupting thunder in each ear.
We see our homes to stubble burn.
 With loved-ones still within, we learn,
 as fearful hearts with terror swell,
that war is hell—oh, war is hell!

To see the fighter's broad brigade,
   where none molest, nor make afraid,
   sweep down, as vultures, from the sun
to cruelly murder everyone,
   the father and son, upon the land,
   the fishers fishing upon the sand,
the boys and girls within the school,
   the wise man, beggar, priest and fool.
   Who ran from death, beneath it fell,
for war is hell—oh, war is hell!

And as each day gives way to night,
   assailing war planes raid and fight,
   the tank, the ship, the missile fire.
The dead in trenches piling higher.
   To hear each painful dying moan,
   as dust makes way to claim its own,
awakes anew the grieving heart.
   The songs of love and bliss depart.
   To all, the tolling of the bell
meant war is hell—oh, war is hell!

So as the foe would bind the free
   and mock the song of liberty,
   so shall the free, by sea and air,
invade the foe, from everywhere!
   In deem of such a worthy cause,
   to enter into Hade's jaws,
relight the torch with freedom's flame
   and conquer all, who kill and maim.
   Let's pray the world recalls it well,
that war is hell—oh, war is hell!

# There Is A Land

There is a land, a good old land,
beneath the sky above,
where honest men are free to work,
and live in peace and love.

There were some men, some valiant men
from the ends of all the earth,
who nobly gave their one and all
to win this country birth.

There is a God, a righteous God,
who long ago ordained
that ne're a king shall rule the land
where only He has reigned.

There is a flag, a grand old flag
that would unite, as one,
some fifty states across this land,
in freedom, proud and strong.

There is a land, a prosperous land
with fields of wheat and corn.
Thank God, who gave us this great land,
the land where I was born!

# Sea Watch

Every day at eventide
I sat beside the sea
and there I marked each sea gull's flight
above in ecstasy.

I saw how none would leave a trail
to witness where they'd been
and none knew whence they were to go,
like many, many men.

I sat and watched the fading reef
descend below the tide,
concealing knives as sharp as steel,
to crush a vessel's side.

I marveled as the sun went down
within the cherry sky
and waved to all the fishing boats,
as they would pass me by.

"Oh where," I wondered, "are they going,
forsaking salty sea,
to family, wife, or loyal friends?
What can they do for me?"

Each day I came at eventide
and rowed to reach the place
where solitude was happiness
and sea gulls soared with grace.

So quiet, peaceful, all alone,
where time was void of strife;
where sea gulls filled the vacancy
of brotherhood in life.

I heard, as waves were whispering
their secrets every day.
I would to tell them to the world,
but kept them hid away.

I heard a heavy rumble
one day, from underneath;
looked up to see a fishing boat
had struck the rocky reef.

A mess of fishermen aboard,
cemented still—from fear—
Their cries had echoed through the dusk,
but no one else was near.

I charged upon my little raft
toward them, as the sky
bestowed upon me heavy clouds
and storms were drawing nigh.

The waves were growing higher
upon the darkened land.
Thank God, I knew those jagged rocks
as though they were my hand.

So there I weaved between the blades
of death, toward them then.
I called within the mounting winds.
I called and called again.

At last, at length, about an hour,
my vessel drawing near,
while waves were warning all of death
I called, and they could hear!

A frightened Frenchman answered me,
the salt within his hair.
A monstrous Welchman clutched his head,
so glad to see me there.

Six men danced upon the beach
from joy, e're rising sun.
But seven, really, reaped rewards
that night, from what I'd done,

For now I sit beside the sea,
as fishers wave again,
and ask myself, "What else is there
that I may do for men?"

# Love and Family

# The Reason I Love You

Amid the vain motives of trouble and sin
and as greed fills the world with despair,
while envy and hate are the rulers of men,
you are the reason I care.

You are the reason I'm living, my love.
The reason I'm breathing is you.
You are the reason I'm reaching above
in all that I say and I do.

You are the reason I waken each day.
You are the reason I sigh.
You are the reason my life is so gay
and so bursting with joy that I cry.

You are the reason I'm seeking the good
out of all that is done, that I see,
and surely the reason, if ever it would,
when I'm kneeling in prayer, isn't me,

For you are the reason that there's goodness and bliss
in my life—and, if ever, I smile.
So truly—the reason I love you—is this:
It's you—that makes living—worthwhile!

# Silence

Not far from the cottage
a grassy hill stood,
wrapped in a cool breeze,
at the edge of the wood.

And often I ventured
alone there to stay,
lonely but happy
at the end of the day.

Nearby the bare hillside
a river once fled.
Hillside's forgotten,
all as if dead.

One drop from the river
was all that was left.
Alone on the hillside
a tree stood, bereft.

Oh, often I went there,
in rain and in shine,
called the hill "Silence"
and claimed it as mine.

I laid on the hillside
and talked to the sun,
"Silence is golden
whenever there's one."

Till one dusk I went there
and failed to return.
Stars I would question
and from them would learn.

"The sunset," they told me
(in quite their own way)
"is only for mourners,
whose hopes soon decay.

For darkness brings sorrow,
you'll lose then your way
and always face grief,
with your back to the day.

Though sunsets are pretty,
they soon lose their sun,
and darkness is sorrow
whenever there's one."

The sunrise was coming
and soon I could see
a hillside of dew,
as bright as could be.

I first saw the river,
filled fresh with its flow.
The hillside still barren,
but wait—did you know

That there on the hillside,
beside the tall tree,
I gazed on another,
as green as could be?

The air felt much fresher.
"Tis a shame," I said then,
"that beauty like this
be known not by men."

A cool breeze a blowing,
and then a reply,
a fair soft young whisper,
"Tis just you and I."

And then there inside me
I felt what was true,
though silence be broken,
whenever there's two.

# Autumn Storm Song

The screen door slamming scares me to bits,
as the wind blows wild outside.
Dogs and chickens are running in fits,
a' searching a place to hide.
The roof-top's leaking, from up on high,
the cold wet Autumn storm.
Come be my love now, lest I die,
keep me dry and warm.

The night outside has been cold and cruel,
as the clouds, they scowl and frown.
A man would be but a gall-darn fool
to watch his barn blow down!
The crop's been molding in the field.
I've nearly lost the farm.
Come by my love, my lovely shield,
keep me dry and warm.

The cattle are standing cold and wet,
blessed with little sense,
Stampede, when lightning strikes, I'll bet.
Tomorrow I'll fix the fence.
The whistling wind, it cracks the glass.
I hope it lasts the night.
Come climb in bed and all will pass,
perhaps, at least, it might.
The tree-limbs toppling upon the house.
T'will keep us safe from harm!
Come love me still, my lovely spouse,
keep me dry and warm!

# Eternal Progression

When you were a spirit and I was a spirit,
eons and eons ago,
before this earth had gained its birth
we frolicked in the heavens aglow,
or resounded with many-a-beautiful note
'mongst the choirs of the spirits of men.
My heart was rife with the joy of life,
for I loved you, even then.

Sinless we lived and sinless we loved
and sinless each day we'd see
our friends go down and win their crown
through trials in mortality.
Anxious, willing and yearning to prove
*we'd* be faithful and true 'till we die,
with a hug and a kiss, we forsook all the bliss
of that spiritual realm in the sky.

Innocent, young and unsullied, our souls
would evolve, through what is called birth,
where spirit and dust together are thrust
to attain our perfection on earth.
Alone and afraid, n'er recalling the past
and our premortal mansions on high,
in this valley of tears, men must search through the years
for their purpose of being—then die.

Seeking to find the companion we loved,
unto whom there were vows made before.
Now if both I and you remain faithful and true,
we'll abide with the Gods evermore.
Renouncing the vile and the blind infidel,
whose heretical theories appall,
we'll pass by the guards, who are keeping the gates,
to our Lord and our God, when He'll call.

Exalted and free, we may dwell with the Gods,
who emit, in their glory, a flame.
In the midst of the skies, we must all harmonize
and become, in our purpose, the same.
So then as we linger at luncheon this day,
o'er many a morsel divine,
let us reminisce when, 'mong the spirits of men,
you vowed *evermore* to be mine!

# The Little Things

I think it's just the little things
that makes me miss her so.
The things like when she burned the toast
or dropped the radio;

Or times like when I went to work,
we always kissed good-bye,
for now I leave an empty house
and only breathe a sigh.

I know it's just the little things,
the things we didn't see,
that really showed my love for her
and showed her love for me.

The things like when I wrecked the car
or she ran out of gas;
or when it cost us twenty bucks
because I drove too fast.

But through it all, we overcame,
with very little strife,
and grew together, one in each,
complements in life.

I smile to think of every time
we sought to help our brother,
for as we both were helping him,
we helped out one another.

Then just recall the major things
we had to overcome
to make our den a happy place
we proudly called our home

Reminds me of romantic tales,
as in the days of yore.
I know when we're together
I'll appreciate her more.

But just to think of what we'd do,
or where we both would go.
I think it's just the little things
that make me miss her so.

# The Proper Tools

So dad, before the winter's in,
you would to build a barn.
You would construct it stout and strong
to weather any storm.
So first you count your building blocks.
You've numbered one and all.
With the layout here
you greatly fear
you've aimed too large or small.
So you pray you've mapped each precious piece
a purpose in the form,
for yes, my man,
it takes a plan
to make it safe and warm!

You check. You have your screwdriver,
your level, wrench and rule,
for you know to do a proper job
it takes the proper tool
and it would be rather difficult
to hammer with a square,
but at the proper time
it's quite sublime
if the proper tool is there.
So you hope you have the hardware,
not haggard, broke or worn,
for you know it takes the proper tools
to build a proper barn!

Now dad, before your life is through,
you would to raise a son.
So first you check your building blocks,
before the job's begun,
and number out his temperaments,
for each is bad or good
and to shape him right,
each day and night,
is the joy of fatherhood.
So you'll pray you've mapped each precious gift
a place, before you're done,
for it always takes a proper plan
to raise a proper son!

You check. You have your discipline.
You've set the proper rule,
for you know to build a proper man
it takes the proper tool
and you know it's rather difficult
to be patient, when he'll swear,
but it's just sublime,
at the proper time,
if the proper tool is there.
Use tolerance and affection,
with example, where you can,
for you know it takes the proper tools
to build a proper man!

## Recollection

We pondered dreams together
 of skies and oceans blue,
Of far off lands and sunsets,
 when all I had was you.

But had those days but lingered
 to dream of lands and sea,
I'd bring them back with gladness
 so you could dream with me!

## Missing Love

I feel your touch each morning
 as darkness leaves its throne
and stroke your hair
 so fine and fair,
but find myself alone.

I smile with you at noontime
 where'ere I seek the shade,
but find at best
 a futile quest
and foolish daydream made.

You lead me to the bedroom
 each night when day is done
and in my sleep
 I hear you weep,
but wake, to find you gone.

# Mother's Mistake

It happened in September,
a day we all shall rue,
when our loving mother got a job
life's treasures to pursue.

Jamie was the oldest,
then Sherry, next in line,
while the third and middle vacancy,
sure enough, was mine.

Then Dan was next in order,
and last, our precious pearl
named Peggy Lee, and all could see
she was her mother's girl.

Our dad was quite a worker,
his salary pretty good,
but with his house filled full of kids,
just made our livelihood.

While nothing new or fancy
we often e'er did see,
but still we loved our happy home.
To this, we all agree,

but never stopped complaining,
as always children do,
to have the same things as our friends.
(And theirs were always new!)

Jamie wanted a bicycle
and sis a store-bought dress
and me, I wanted an archery set
and it *had* to be the best!

Dan, he needed a coat and shoes,
but Peg, then nicknamed "Muffin,"
when asked what she was craving for
replied her casual "nuffin."

While Mom, she dreamt of having
a pretty winter shawl
and Dad, he didn't like the thought
of her working—not at all,

but deep inside was thinking
(Which he later did confess.)
to get him now a set of tools
would save much weariness!

So Mom, she went exploring
for a job, as day begun
and took li'l "Muffin" by her side,
and soon she found her one!

So Mother started working
each day from eight to four
and bought the things we had to have
and many, many more.

But home, it seemed so empty,
once filled with warmth and love.
We used to find Mom's counsel there,
but now the streets did rove.

And precious little "Muffin"
was still so sore afraid,
though for her care, "just one more year,"
Mom hired for her a maid.

And Mom came home so tired,
no longer "glad to see"
her kids come home from school each day
at quarter after three.

Father got home later,
expecting there to find
a loving wife's awaiting arms;
too oft were words unkind.

So home, it grew much bleaker.
Though "Muffin" noticed first,
we all know now, with deep remorse,
it hurt our Jamie worst.

For then he started doing
the things he oughtn't do,
and his friends were friends, due to her work,
that Mother never knew.

It seems but from that moment
she n'er could him control
and Satan swayed at a meager price
her Jamie's priceless soul.

At last, Mom passed the bedroom
one night, as day was done,
and heard her "Muffin" say her prayers
and thus her prayer begun:

"My Father, Dear, in heaven,
I pray that Mom will see
the trouble now our family's in.
Please bring her home to me!

For Jamie's sore in trouble
and everyone so cold!
Please bring back Mommy to us now,
the shepherdess of our fold.

We miss her so much, Father,
so bring her back again
that we may share her loving care.
In Jesus' name. Amen."

So while inside the bedroom
a daughter prayed for grace,
outside the door her mother dear
regained her rightful place.

And from that very moment
resumed her duties plain,
and never once did Mother
forsake her home again!

So, if you have to, mothers,
(And not from worldly lust,)
then work again, but only when
you absolutely must!

# Home's The Place

You may search in unknown lands
or visit a tropic isle,
but bid me not to come along,
for I'll just sit and smile.
You may explore antarctic wastes,
but ask me not to roam,
for nowhere else will suit my tastes,
nowhere else, but home.

For nowhere else in all the world
is a family like mine.
Nowhere else do I like the food
every time I dine.
Nowhere else do I have a house
or a child that loves me so,
a sweet and tender-hearted spouse
that would die to see me go.

You may be in Lexington,
or as far away as Rome.
You may tour in Switzerland,
but please, just leave me home.
You may visit Paris, too,
or go to Germany.
That may just be the place for you,
but home's the place for me!

# Dissatisfied

Girls, from about the age of four,
(When boys, still filled with dread
observe them play their girlish games.)
are longing to be wed
to their handsome prince,
they call him then,
but soon in times to come
they'll call their charming Cyrano
a no-good dirty bum.

And boys, they hold their peace, somehow,
'till she enters in the room
at about sixteen and filled out well,
—then longs to be the groom
of his "princess dear,"
he calls her then,
so well inclined to brag,
but soon he'll call his royal queen
a no-good screaming nag.

And neither, while they live at home,
appreciate their mother,
their father (as the routine goes),
their sister or their brother,
but as is true
with most, I guess,
who hurry, fear and fret
themselves into their wedding vows,
they afterwards regret.

For neither are impeccable
(To this we may agree.)
and both have idiosyncrasies
which both had failed to see
in each other yet,
but still must learn
harsh words to yet refrain,
for in the cold and bitter truth
they cause each other pain.

And soon it comes that many souls
their marriage do deplore.
So as they wished they were so long,
they now desire no more!
And oh it's sad
that joy in life
they never could be taught.
Happiness is to live and love
exactly what you've got!

# Surrounding Our Supper Table

Oh were I back, when I was young
and through my boyhood wending,
with sister and brother
and father and mother
all, as a family, blending!
For there was a time
that came each day
when each was as loving as able,
for there was where
I learned to care,
surrounding our supper table!

It was an oasis, a harbor of rest,
where we each other's triumphs were cheering.
With applause for our merit,
we soon would inherit
a concern for another, endearing.
T'was seldom a word
bringing anger or strife
that would split that sweet spirit asunder
for, when discord arose,
dad would follow, to close,
as the lightning is followed by thunder.

If someone did wrong and father found out,
the correction was never impending,
nor wrath nor fury,
nor judge nor jury,
nor cause for a council defending
around that place,
that safe abode,
where the food was but served with affection.
I'm saying to you
it was tried and it's true,
for it sent us the proper direction!

So now, as we're older, with kids of our own,
we'd raise them the best we are able,
so we try but to share
of that same spirit there,
surrounding our supper table!

# Spring Sowing

I remember well the days at home
and the winter nights, so cold.
There were many a song
round the heart-stone fire
and many a story told.
And in the spring, when the snow was gone,
Dad would say, when the sowing began,
"It's not the man that makes the work,
but the work that makes the man."

So he plowed the rows as well as he could,
to make them look straight, when sown.
Many a field he plowed o'er again,
too ashamed to call them his own.
Though Mom, she would tell him he worked too hard,
he made her his greatest fan.
"For it isn't the man that shapes the work, Ma,
It's the work that shapes the man!"

And there was the time that the flood-gate broke
and bathed, in the harvest moon,
the corn, the oats and the patch of peas;
we toiled all night, through noon.
But Dad just said, as he always would,
that it must have been part of the plan;
for it isn't the man that makes the work,
but the work that makes the man.

And then came the day I left our home,
for a home of my own to form.
I talked with Dad, as we walked the fields,
and felt his arm, so warm,
as he told me whatever I do in life
to do the best I can,
for it isn't the man that makes the work,
it's the work that makes the man!

# Snapshot

I quickly snapped her picture once again
to capture on my daughter's face a precious grin.
A priceless frozen glimpse was given me
to cherish so, throughout eternity.
For when she grows so beautiful and tall,
this is what I'll keep and that is all.
For only but a shortened little while
may still I yet adore her infant smile,
bestowing to me now, I do confide,
the richest blessing here, a father's pride.
I kneel to pray and thank my God above
for the richest happiness, a father's love.
So then, with this, I must be e'er content.
Her treasured infant smile, so innocent,
may not be yet tomorrow, as today,
as all things must and will yet pass away.
To hold this pose but still a little while
and capture on the print her precious smile
and see behind those eyes a spirit there,
which brings to me a joy beyond compare,
for I, as yet her father, so can see
inside her sunny soul, a part of me!

# Arrival

It's been a long two years
in a far off land,
but finally now it's past.
As the big jet plane
descends again,
I'm back home at last.

There's mom and dad
and sis and Fred
and the girl I still adore.
Handshakes, kisses,
tears and hugs,
for I'm back home once more!

It's been a long two years
and so much has changed
in the town I called my own.
But, spite all fears
these last two years
I, myself, have grown.

I think of all
I left behind,
as memories do downpour,
Friendships, customs,
food and dress,
foreign folk and lore.

It's been a long two years
and the lonely nights
are the nights I so deplore!
But now I see
it ecstasy
to be back home once more!

# To Give Her Daughter Forevermore

A daughter came to her mom at home
and her eyes were wet that night.
She held a ring within her hand
and, for a burden, fright.
"He says he wants to marry me,"
her quivering lips outbroke.
She looked at her mother's silent face
and fancied that she spoke.

"He owns a house and a piece of land
and has a job in town."
The mother's eyes were on the floor
at the hem of her daughter's gown.
"I even think that I love him, Mom.
He's really quite a man.
Tell me what I should do," she said,
"tell me, if you can."

The mother looked up and only smiled
and held her daughter there
and wished a silver spoon for her lips
and a golden pin for her hair.
Without the door, the young man stood
and longed for the dream of his heart,
Though she was bound to her mom with an iron band
he would tear those two apart.

The mother thinks it little to let
him take her where he would,
a tender kiss for the young at heart,
she knew she always could.
But to *give* her daughter *forevermore*
to a strange, but goodly man,
she prays them both much happiness
and only hopes she can!

# Take Hold My Hand

Take hold my hand
my child, my son,
as through the storm we stride.
The walk is short,
but yet so long,
so stay here by my side.
Impetuous feet, with heedless eyes,
may stumble o'er a stone.
So hold my hand, my child, my son,
until, at last, you're grown.

Take hold my hand,
my child, my boy,
and let me be your guide.
You're just not yet
accountable,
so please, stay near my side.
I hear the tempest's howling gusts,
as limbs from trees are blown.
So hold my hand, my child, my boy,
until at last, you're grown.

Take heed, beware
my child, my son,
as you the storm must face.
Your footsteps leave
your tracks behind,
which no man can erase.
When you're at last accountable,
you'll reap the seeds you've sown.
I'll do my best to mark the way—
but then you're on your own.

# On The Light Side

# Indebted

That time of month is here once more.
My cursed mail I do deplore
and wonder why they even say
I must meet sums I cannot pay,
for out of near and out of far
come falling bills, like a falling star,
demanding sums I do not know,
for worn-out things of long ago.
It really makes for quite a show!

And so I read each sad report,
which threatens me they'll go to court
and when I pass the stores each day
the cashiers turn their backs away.
Oh what a rotten man I am!
Why I'd trade debts with Uncle Sam!
(But never would, I truly feel—
I've never been inclined to steal
and he'd lose out on such a deal!)

So as I gaze, with every bill
my heart does more with horror fill.
A thousand worries find me then,
(Until they want it back again.)
It's broken now, so I just say,
"I don't want it anyway!"
But then they say, "So now we know!
We'll just have to let it go,
so keep it please, we want your dough!"

So on went life—the world, it turned,
during which I my credit cards burned!
With all my cash devoured away,
I'll soon be even, I can say
then gaze on back and heave a sigh
and look my debtors in the eye.
With ulcers sown, from deep regret,
I've learned a lesson, you can bet,
to stay forever out of debt!

# Uninformed

I've meant to for sometime, my dear...
you know, it's plain to see
that you have rather grown right here,
in fact, enormously!

I've wanted to express to you,
as I your lips caressed,
that this has caused me problems too.
In fact, I'm quite embarrassed!

Why, just last week our guests were in.
As they were sitting there,
they whispered how you once were thin.
I loathed to see them stare!

My gentle love, I know you know.
Let's take this time to talk
and soon you'll be just like you were.
(We'll jog around the block!)

A push-up and a sit-up too,
with these we may begin,
and sooner than you grew and grew
you'll be fragile, frail and thin!

The hospital, you're telling me.
You say your tummy aches?
And from its size, I'd think it would,
my dear, for heaven's sakes!

The labor room? Now what's in there
to help a girl like you?
Of all the things in this whole world
a man could misconstrue!

# Thank Heavens For Bossy!

Try to conceive, if you are able,
A pitcher of milk upon your table
And try to conceive, if you know how,
A huge red barn and a young brown cow.

Soon before the day gets warmer,
In the barn comes a cow and a bright young farmer.
And soon, before you know it, as smooth as silk,
In the sanitized container flows fresh white milk.

Milk for your headache, milk for your sneeze,
Milk for your yogurt, milk for your cheese,
Milk for your muscles to keep them alert,
Milk for your ice-cream to have as dessert.

Soon comes the dairy truck, the milk to retrieve
And now please, a dairy plant, try to conceive.
The milk's tested gently, so much is it prized,
And now it is ready to be homogenized.

Straight to the cartons then it must flow
And fresh to the grocer soon it shall go.
The milk for the ice cream, the milk for the butter,
The milk for the sour cream, it makes my heart flutter.

The milk in the yogurt, the milk in the cheese—
In a humble sense of gratitude I drop to my knees
And thank all the heavens as well as I know how
For milk, cheese, and butter—and Bossy, the cow!

# Poor Old Sam!

My heart goes out
and skips a perk
for poor Sam Jones,
our District clerk.
He always sees the rising sun
and never quits till day is done.
He always misses all the fun!

He writes with lead;
he writes with ink;
he writes until
his fingers stink!
He types it once. He types it twice.
He does his work so clean and nice.
I think he pays an awful price!

And poor old Sam,
so pale and weak.
There's no one
with his physique!
While I play ball with all the men,
he plays ball still once again.
But his ball comes on a ball point pen!

My heart goes out
for the lonely jerk,
to each and every
District clerk,
who has it bad as bad can be,
except when comes eternity—
and then I'll wish that jerk was me!

# Fair Weather Saint

On Sunday morn
a storm is born
and in August it is snowing,
to give some moose
a good excuse
why he should not be going
to Sunday School
As is the rule
when things aren't fine and dandy
and life's not sweet,
he just won't eat,
until they serve some candy.

Don't say he ain't
a goodly saint,
because he's not attending.
He's really nice,
but sacrifice
he never was befriending.
When rain, it falls
he hugs the walls,
for he's really learned to fear it
and so the bum
just doesn't come
and loses then the spirit.

And though the rain
will n'er refrain,
throughout the Sabbath streaking,
the one who'd start
to touch his heart
is at the pulpit, speaking.
But he never heard
a single word
at home, on sacrificing
and so the guy
stays warm and dry
and lives on cake and icing!

(Oh, by the way,
  I forgot to say
  though now he has it easy,
when judgment's here
  he'll greatly fear
  and things won't be so breezy,
for on the latch
  there's still a catch
  that will always be impressing.
The one who'll go,
  mid rain or snow,
  is the one who'll reap the blessing!)

# A Visit From Uncle Sam

He looked like quite a codger,
old man round eighty five;
we marvelled how he stayed so strong
or how he e'er survived
as he walked along the roadside,
but he stopped at our front door
and asked if he might stay the night,
though he n'er was seen before,
with his stove-pipe hat and log coat-tails
he appeared like quite a ham
and, when he calmly introduced himself,
he claimed he was "Uncle Sam"!

We tried to keep from smiling,
when he told us his aged name,
that he formerly was the founder
of its once great power and fame.
"And though our Land may be getting old,
men shan't to think t'will fail,
for, though Uncle Sam may be aging some,
he's strong as an iron rail"!

He claimed he was a witness
of the bloody civil war,
"shook hands with mister Lincoln,
before his life was o'er."
and we wondered, as we talked to him,
if it was truth, or just a sham,
if the man who stood before us,
was really our "Uncle Sam."

He told us there were many a time
men claimed our Land would fall,
with princes, kings and majesties
surrounding our country all,
but we learned that night, when he stayed with us,
our Land's not weak and frail!
For, though "Uncle Sam" may be aging some,
he's strong as an iron rail!

# Lesson Number 56,529

Red means stop and green means go.
These two things, I surely know!
But when the light turns on between,
I don't see red and I don't see green.
They tell me all it means is slow,
so I just guess that that means go!
For when I let up on the gas,
the guy behind will try to pass,
then decide to not, instead,
and by this time the light's turned red!

So there I am, bored to tears,
waiting there a million years.
It's green, at last! My heart does stir
and soon I'm off at sixty-per!
When just ahead, there I see
a yellow signal staring me.
Recalling then my brakes are worn,
I hit the gas and blow my horn!
I made it, whew! I'm good I know,
until I hear a siren blow.

So soon I'm begging on my knees,
pleading mercy and asking "Please!"
But as he writes my address down,
he looks at me and scowls a frown
and says "From now on you will learn
when e'er you see the signal turn!"

He hands me papers brown, like fudge,
telling me to see the judge
and on the very bottom line
big black numbers state the fine.
That, or else six months in jail.
My heart begins to weep and wail.
Convinced my driving is a flop,
I know that yellow *now* means STOP!

# Chess

I would the weary one confess
who made mankind the game of chess
and caused so much unhappiness.
I'm sure if he could yet but see
he'd alter it a bit for me.

I'd really like to meet the snook
who thought there needs must be a rook,
whose tricky moves could fill a book.
His morbid mind must thought it merry.
(By no means was it necessary!)

And then perhaps perceive his plight,
whose pleasures pioneered the knight.
(To make one so just isn't right.)
I'm sure if he could see it yet
his heart would heave in deep regret.

And I can't conceive that he couldn't care,
who put the bishop beside him there.
I just don't think that that was fair!
I'm sure that now, if he were me,
he'd look again and soon agree!

He must have nearly lost his bean,
who gave such power to the queen.
There's many times she's wiped me clean!
It's pure injustice of the louse.
(His mother must have ruled the house!)

And then the pawn, (We're almost through!)
there's very little he can do,
so I guess that he is worthless too!
Take these away and let's begin,
so maybe *finally* I can win!

## Second Thoughts

I ask, with this modern-day pen,
why God gave so much knowledge to men,
but I guess in His heart,
when the world's blown apart,
He'll decide not to do it again!

## The Extra Mile

There once was a bishop named Clyde,
who fell from a steeple and died,
And no one knows why,
(I must say, with a sigh)
he was called on, last week, to preside!

## Promises, Promises, Promises!

There once was a father, named John,
Who died, while a-mowing his lawn,
For his boys (in the shade)
All promised him aid,
But when it came time to *work*—they were gone!